D1361319

A Commonplace Book of Pie

A Commonplace Book of Pie

by Kate Lebo

with illustrations by
Jessica Lynn Bonin

CHIN MUSIC
PRESS

A Chin Music Press original
Chin Music Press, Inc.
2621 24th Ave W.
Seattle, WA 98199-3407
USA
www.chinmusicpress.com

"Lemon Meringue" originally appeared in the summer 2013 issue of Gastronomica magazine.
Printed in the USA.
Library of Congress Cataloguing-in-Publication data is available.

"If you wish to make an apple pie from scratch,
you must first invent the universe."

— Carl Sagan

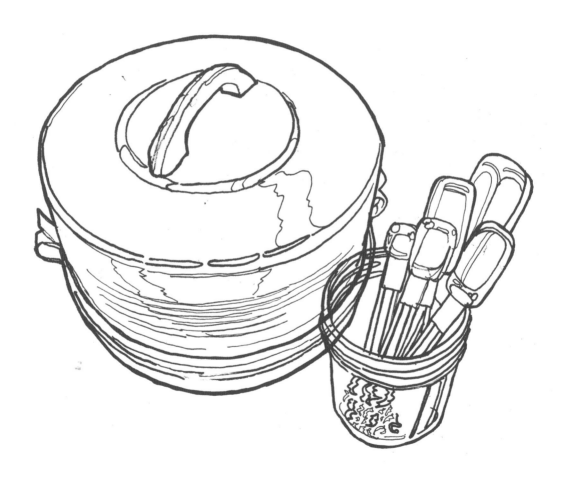

Before You Begin

The difference between superlative pie and a wish for cake is crust. Understand that pie is a generous but self-centered substance. It likes attention, not affection. Do not hug your crust. Do not rub its back or five its high. Don't fuss with refrigerators every step of the way. Keep the water and butter cold, and remember what a wise baker once said: The goal is pie.

Pie is best

a) hot

b) cold

c) with whip

d) a la mode

e) all of the above

What's your favorite?

Apple Pie

Banana Cream Pie

Blackberry Pie

Blueberry Pie

Cherry Pie

Chocolate Cream Pie

Coconut Cream Pie

Cranberry Pie

Key Lime Pie

Lemon Meringue Pie

Lemon Shaker Pie

Lingonberry Pie

Mincemeat Pie

Mud Pie

Mumbleberry Pie

Orange Cream Pie

Peach Pie

Peanut Butter Pie

Pecan Pie

Plum Pie

Pumpkin Pie

Raspberry Pie

Rhubarb Custard Pie

Strawberry Rhubarb Pie

Vanilla Cream Pie

Rules of Thumb

1. Share your pie.

2. Never promise to make pie and fail to deliver on that promise.

3. Do not cut pie while it is still hot or the filling won't set properly. It is okay to break smaller pieces of the crust off for taste-testing purposes.

4. Do not put a butter crust pastry pie in the refrigerator. Refrigeration ruins pastry and introduces off-flavors.

5. Do refrigerate your pie, regardless of pastry type, if it contains significant quantities of dairy.

6. When making crust, the butter must be cold. This bears repeating.

7. The butter must be cold.

8. The water you use to make pie dough must be icy cold. Ensure frigidity by filling a cup with water, adding three ice cubes, and freezing it while preparing the flour and fat.

9. When serving pie, do not smash your crust between a chef's knife and fork, or gouge it with a spoon, or balance it on the blade of a butter knife. Use a pie server.

10. Pies can take four hours to make. Forgive the pie maker her tardiness.

Facts of Pie

"We ought to make the pie higher."

— George W. Bush

"Rilke was devoted to polishing furniture. Jackson Pollock baked pies."

— David Markson

Pumpkin

Contrary to popular opinion, pumpkin pie-lovers are adventurous, quizzical, good in bed and voluminously communicative. No need to ask a pumpkin pie-lover if he'll call ahead for reservations. He'll arrive at the restaurant early, order a drink and have the waitstaff in his fan club before you get off work. By the time you arrive he might even have the hostess's number. Do not trust him to say the right thing to your parents; do trust him to charm your friends. Consider for a moment a can of Libby's pumpkin puree, how a pumpkin does not have a choice, but if it did, it could become a porchlight or a smear on the street. It could be hollowed and hallowed and filled with soup and served in a bistro to people who do not smash pumpkins. It could rot, unsold, in the field, or fill this can of future pie. Do you see now why pumpkin pie is not boring? If it were, more people would know how to talk to bartenders.

Mincemeat

Only one woman alive today would say her favorite pie is mincemeat. She makes hers with green tomatoes and mixed assorted meat-stuffs. Her grandchildren hide her slices in their mouths and spit them into milk glasses when she gets up to answer the telephone. *No thank you. Now is not a good time.* She wanted to be a writer. She took photographs and painted, wore Isadora colored scarves that covered her hair like hair, was the most beautiful woman in town and justifiably vain. She likes to imagine her movements as gusts of wind blowing her children around the world, her little boats.

Blueberry

Children are born to devour what's set before them, especially on factory tours. In Crayola factories, wax cools in cylindric wrappings while plastic-eyed field trippers fill their goggles with inedible hue. But what does this have to do with pie in the sky, antioxidants, or the favorite breakfast of certain birds? Blueberries burst beneath teeth and heat all the same, so you'd never know the pale of their innards. The blueberry pie-lover knows. To him, a pert slice and a little lemon is the difference between wanting to view paradise and viewing it.

Lingonberry

The Swedish have a word for hunger that sounds like ice before it's scraped off a windshield and, when held in the mouth, glints like a metal tooth. The lingonberry pie-lover is like this word, so he collects antique orthodontia and cultivates peculiar hungers. The scent of gasoline evaporating from asphalt, the sneer of grass on a good dress. Being told *no* or *slow down* when in proximity of food makes the lingonberry pie-lover capable of aggravated misdemeanors. I don't suggest testing this assertion.

Chocolate Cream

People who love chocolate cream pie move through this world in a swarm of music. Their cars leak basslines; their exhaust sings from the dark of the pipe. Periodically they experiment with the softness of their genders and find them lacking every time, wear skirts to feel the hair on their thighs and pants to bind their bodies into the clean lines of a park bench. They invite you to sit down. The chocolate pie-lover would like to convince you that her height is three inches above the crown of her head. She isn't lying, exactly. She's creating the truth, believer by believer, just as you would if you too had a voice as big as a church.

Lemon Meringue

Legend has it lemon meringue pie was invented by the Sisters of the Holy Names the day after their first night in Portland, Oregon. On the day of the invention of lemon meringue pie, clouds gathered overhead, all threat and no spit, just a cluster of gray over sun. Back east, the sisters had heard tales of Exodus-style rains, flooding until the future courthouse and city hall were specks of marble flotsam only God could pinch from the froth. Sister Maria in her tent, contemplating a month of daylight darkness ahead, remembered the seven lemons in her trunk. She squeezed them into yolks and sugar, then poured the filling into an improvised crust of crackers. Taking inspiration from her new home's dour weather, she beat sweetened egg whites until they puffed like clouds and gently piled them over the bright yellow filling, obscuring it from view.

The sisters loved her creation and fought for the biggest pieces. Sister Maria disliked the sound of raised voices, so she walked into the woods to leave the din behind. As she peered through dripping firs for a glimpse of construction further upriver, she thought about God and said, "You don't want pie in the sky when you die. You want something here on the ground while you're still around."

Years later, unbeknownst to them both, Muhammad Ali would say the exact same thing after winning a fight in Miami. The sisters campaigned to make this aphorism the motto of the school for girls they planned to construct, and though Home Economics is considered unfeminist and unfashionable these days, some still think that St. Mary's Academy for Girls should complement their rigorous math and science courses with a lesson on how to whip the perfect whites.

Cherry

We have formed our impressions of this most American pie on canned filling. Which is more American? Processed fruit in explosive syrup, or sweating in the sun while balancing on a slender ladder? Each July the cherry pie-lover gathers hard red fruits in her dress until the moment she needs her right hand for balance, then lets go, spills her harvest in the grass where birds can eat the mess. She likes sun hats, tolerates baseball, and does not go to church, but prays when she is afraid of failure or death.

Peanut Butter

If you love peanut butter pie, you are either Dolly Parton or someone who loves her.

Peach

All peach pie-lovers are men, if only on the inside. I met a peach pie-lover from Seattle once. She said that adding cayenne to cinnamon and consuming it in a peach pie will make you grow hair on your palms. Some people are scared to love peach pie for this very reason. Those who aren't afraid join a long line of people who know that there is nothing more delicious than loving what you fear. Even if desire makes you undesirable. Even if it grows a beard on your high five.

Vanilla Cream

If vanilla cream pie is your favorite, you probably also like horses, getting lost in your hometown, abandoned houses, farmers markets, insensible shoes, and double-tall lattes with a splash of, well, you know.

Apple

Apple pie invented itself on the outskirts of what would become Hoboken, New Jersey on the afternoon of August 5, 1717. The apple orchards, too, were accidental, carried afar in the bellies of birds and bears and other four-legged fruit-eating animals, the seeds polished and shined by the intestines of their hosts and planted in spoor on new ground. When apple trees began to blossom among the inedible deciduous woods, settlers raced to cut the alders and underbrush away so the apples could have the full portion of sunlight they hoped their God owed them.

Back then, apple trees did not fruit every year. The settlers blamed themselves for this: in their greed, they had picked the first apple trees to near death. That the trees chose to hibernate every other year seemed an act of self preservation. The settlers resolved to be patient.

1717 was an off year, so a farm wife named Nancy Cottonwood retrieved a basket of apples stored in her cellar from the previous harvest. In the cool darkness the apples had kept remarkably well, but were no longer attractive. To appease their vanity, she cut them up. To honor their barren parents, she removed the tough core and seeds. And because it was the day before Sunday, her day of rest, she made pastry instead of slow-rising brown bread, wrapped the apples so they would not get cold, and baked them in her wood-burning oven. When William Cottonwood returned from the fields, he smelled his dinner on the windowsill and said, "Wife, give me a kiss. Food without hospitality is medicine." It was a proverb he had heard in the tavern in town, where apple cider ran cleaner than water from any well in this would-be virgin world his people had claimed by calling it *new*.

Plum

In plum country, landlords own houses but not the trees that twist their yards into piles of light breakfast. Their leases include flecked black canning pots as wide and deep as stoves; the last page grants harvest rights to *Renter* if she recruits her own crows to pick the fallen clean. She has grown out of her father's house but not his dinner dictums, so *Take all you want but eat all you take* turns April's greed of blossoms into August's tyranny of plums. Her fingers are blued by Italian prunes she rushes into jam and suspends in honey before the fruit can wrinkle into rot. She'll sweeten bread with her labor all winter, and vote for a mayor who believes plum pie is a currency that should be traded, never sold, especially between the treed and treeless.

Cranberry

You dare not trust yourself to make the house pleasant with your wit and so you buy ice cream. Hello cranberry pie-lover. Your lights are light because your darks are dark, bog-like, ballooned. Where your rivers break into lakes, weeds silk the dark water. Do you wonder how it feels to back-float in a cranberry field, cerise fruit bubbling up your arms' lazy windmill? What would cranberries sound like, their million submerged collisions? Like a tub of loose beads? A handful of lost change chattering in the dirt? The bite of tart fruit loses its teeth *a la mode*—but why speak of it? You're too adult to chew open mouthed, yet this pie is more vivid under the light of a loose jaw, a little air.

Strawberry Rhubarb

A marriage of convenience that lucked into love. I'd like to meet you on your wedding day, poured into a delicate dress and shaking with the weight of the unknown. I want to see the strange face of your groom lit with conjugal dread, the purse of his lips as he leans in to learn how to kiss, the yield and stop of your painted mouth, so careful. You each held mouthfuls of pearls. I want to watch the moment your dread met his. How the first clutch of feeling transformed into fear and you began to understand that fear is a scout for your soul's journey toward what it truly wants. You faced the crowd for the first time together, hand in hand, and walked into the sum of your new life, a new name to bind you.

Rhubarb Custard

The woman who serves rhubarb custard pie is queen of the tealit dining room, her whisperclean countertops formica bright. Though she has been known to fake orgasms, she would never serve Splenda to guests. Her smile can stretch criticism into compliments and put a man in the wrong for being born without dimples. She knows rhubarb is a vegetable but lets it pretend otherwise. Doesn't mind when the Washington State Rhubarb Coalition cross-dresses it in custard and plates it quivering pale, lukewarm to the fork. Of the forgivenesses available for use by the average human, hers is the kind that would rather be wrong than rude.

Shaker Lemon

Often overlooked in favor of lemon meringue, Shaker lemon pie is not a housewife's treat so much as a grandmother's indulgence. The recipe is as easy to remember as a cliché: slice two lemons paper thin, macerate in two cups sugar overnight, beat four eggs and gently stir into lemon-sugar, add filling to crust, bake, bam. The sort of recipe that finds a flat surface in the brain and settles for life. Those who prefer Shaker lemon pie above all other pies get immense satisfaction from organizing pantries, cleaning closets, gathering earthquake kits, proselytizing the importance of being prepared. When the big one hits, the Shaker lemon pie-lover knows that the difference between safety and panic will be a quart of filtered water, a chocolate bar, a pack of smokes, a deck of cards, a companion to hug on the floor.

Coconut Cream

I know the urge to shove your face into this cirrus-soft offer is sometimes stronger than stainless steel, but this is the table. You must maintain your composure. Try welding yourself to the sensible handle of a hotel fork. Say heaven is an all-night diner next door to the realm's best booze hall and pulltab lounge. Coconut cream pie is what sinners are served the moment before the manager stalks from the kitchen to eighty-six the lot of you. *Inappropriate!* he swears, sweat-faced. Glass doors yawn on their bells to unadmit you, to keep your pie. Sneaking in was worth a shot, I guess. If only a shave and a shower had the power to forgive. Then you'd be in business.

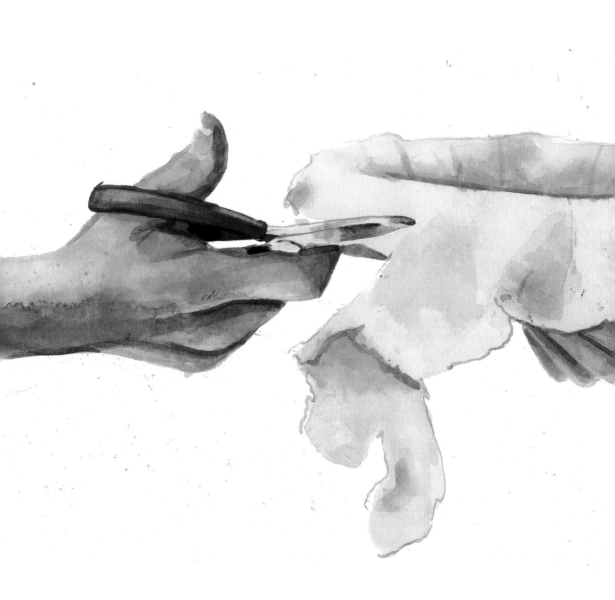

Key Lime

When Annie Dillard writes, "Any instant the sacred may wipe you with its finger," she means key lime pie. Which is dust, which is bone, which (according to Dillard) smells like pie. With which finger does the sacred wipe? Don't ask the key lime pie-lover. He works fast so he might deserve rest, reads hard so he might invent stories, beats his own time in one-man pie eating contests so citrus will make the gutters of his mouth sing. The finger that wipes his lips is his.

Mud

Those who prefer mud pie also prefer jeans, but that much should be obvious. There's a horse or two in her past, a neighbor's whiskered grass chewer or a frizzy pony tethered on the wrong side of a chain link fence where she tests her fingers' reach, her unrotten apples. A goat won't do. When parents yell and sisters pinch, when safety locks her in the house all August until even her marrow is air conditioned, she thinks about that horse. The Amish have a saying, *If someone throws mud in your face, let it dry. It will fall off.* This pie-lover likes that idea. Not to turn the other cheek but to bore her gaze full into the slap, to wither it with attention, to ride that dirt into the ground.

Raspberry

In stilettos the raspberry pie-lover is Barbie-toed and steel-footed, a mystery of high heels and eyeshadow. Her talents have never been under her control, so she takes pride in them as often as she regrets what they are not, wears her confidence with a spike heel. She understands better than most how far a form can stray from its intended purpose once beauty gets involved, knows her mother's warning by head and by heart: wear the shoe long enough and it will bend the bones to fit.

Orange Cream

You are an invention of the modern age, *sui generis*, or so you'd like to believe. Your precocious tongue ties birds to their beaks and scares the child you would protect with its lashings. The child is you, sweetness. Orange foam doesn't rhyme with *mousse à l'orange*, nothing does. Not garage, storage, fromage, hinge, geranium or ayatollah. Say "navel" with me ten times fast.

Pecan

Only those who will live longer than they expected to can truly love pecan pie, which doesn't explain its status as death row's most requested last dessert, or why chopped pecans, corn syrup, directions from the Karo bottle's cherry-red side are what mercy tastes like to some. But there you have it. Carrie's cinematic pigs' blood was made of the same stuff (sans crust and nuts), plus a tub of pigment to sweeten her psychic gore. An outsider's inside story. Other pecan pie-lovers manage their fear of the future by playing as hard as they work. They distract themselves from the deadlines of birthdays with the sweetest of sweet pies, honey upon brown sugar, molasses upon fat. A pecan pie-lover prepares for the worst with dessert, and does not share.

Mumbleberry

When the mumbleberry pie-lover's non-compliance with narrative unity is outlawed by Turkish courts, she's thrown into a fantasy gulag with William S Burroughs and his jewelry box of multi-use needles. He sews her a coat from pages of *The Soft Machine*, stacks of which shove the ceiling from the wall and the wall from the window. It's cold down there, but better conversation can't be found. She believes in excessive moderation; he pastors his church of regret so poorly that nonbelievers press ears to the bars of his cell to reinforce their refusals to convert. Will you comfort me with apples? he asks his new roommate. Of course, she says. Slice by slice, we'll serve our sentences.

Banana Cream

Bad bananas are like push-up bras—a promise of tenderness can deliver tasteless mush and we're not supposed to complain. And the filling. Will it be vanilla or caramel? Coconut or butterscotch? The difference is a matter of importance to our lover, indifference to everyone else. Banana cream pie-lovers appreciate the sum of their parts, so they enjoy the unphotogenic angles of their love: the crumb mess, the toothache wakefulness, warm nights of weakness spent sugarbuzzed. They think a full and quiet mouth is a statement of joy jeweled as a copper penny on the blue bottom of a June pool. When the banana cream pie-lover quotes "promises and pie crust are made to be broken," he means bananas are forgivable, fallible as God intended, and cream is desire left over after what you expected proves to be smaller and closer than it originally appeared.

Blackberry

Says deathless Emerson: The eye can't satisfy unless it has a horizon. In the place you grew up, where was yours? How far could you see? Was there a road by your house? Where did it lead? To eradicate blackberry brambles, one must believe in rhizomes. What was your first encounter with a wild animal? How far were you allowed to roam? You'll know a plant is non-native if it's called invasive. In what sort of landscape do you feel safest? Where do you belong?

Recipes

"Science means simply the aggregate of all the recipes that are always successful. All the rest is literature."

— Paul Valery

Notes on Pie

The Ice Water Method

Best. Trust the tap and freezer to provide the most effective binding agents at the right price. Fill a spouted cup with water and ice, freeze it while you make the fat-flour, and dribble it over the mixture. I listen to my wrist when I'm pouring. Don't ask me for tablespoons. They are beyond my ability.

The Boiling Water Method

Exists. Pork pies and occasional grandmothers require it. I don't understand how it works. The object of the ice water is to preserve fat chunks. Boiling water melts them to slurry. I include this method only to inform you that it is an option, especially if you want to be old-fashioned, British, or contrary.

The Vodka Method

Works best if you keep a fifth in the freezer at all times. Part of pie's charm is its economy—when you can, at any home-moment, make the split decision to pie-bake. This requires the constant presence of all ingredients in the home. I don't know about you, but in my house a bottle of vodka doesn't last long.

On Lard

If you've been using all-butter or a butter-Crisco combo in your crusts, try lard immediately. Your dough will bake into ethereal joy.

On Butter

Unsalted is best. Good quality is recommended—European butter has a lower water content. That is to say, there's more butter in their butter.

On Crisco

Don't think about it. I mean, use it (angelic flakes, long shelf life, cheap) but don't think about what you're doing to your trans-fats levels. When it stubbornly resists detaching from a spoon, even under hot water, don't think about the dark of your arteries. When it leaves a translucent greasy residue not unlike vaseline, don't think about what veins truck to your heart. On the bright side, it's vegetarian and—according to Industrial Revolution-era ads—pure as light.

On Flour

King Arthur brand is best. Remember to stir the bag before scooping the cup to aerate packed flour.

On Making Dough

Use a light touch, go by feel. For more help, see the following recipe.

On Refrigeration

Key, but not to be overestimated. Fat should stay chilled but not frozen so that, when rubbed into flour, it retains its form. Butter chunks become marbling when the dough is rolled. Marbling becomes flakes when the pie bakes. Freezing the fat will make it too hard.

Chilled water helps fat stay cool as it turns into dough. Frozen water is ice, which won't make dough at all.

Fussy bakers would tell you to refrigerate dry ingredients. As a general rule, I disagree with fussiness.

On Wax Paper

If you are new to pie-making, if the dough is too delicate or dry, if the dough is old or defrosted (which tends to dry it out), roll the dough on wax paper. Place a large sheet on a flat surface, sprinkle flour in a wide circle, and roll the dough to $1/8$ inch thickness. It may sneak over the sides of the paper. That is okay. To place a bottom crust in a pie plate, flip it over, center it, and peel off the wax paper at a sharp angle. A wide angle will tear the dough. To place a top crust on a pie, flip it over, center it on the filling, and peel off the wax paper at a sharp angle.

On the Counter

My preferred method. Saves paper, time, and requires a little courage. To roll out dough on a counter, sprinkle flour liberally on a flat surface, place the dough disc in the middle of the flour patch, hit it squarely with the rolling pin a few times to flatten it a little, and commence rolling. Every couple rolls, slide a pastry scraper underneath the dough and rotate it slightly to ensure that the dough won't stick. When it is 6 to 8 inches wide, flip the entire thing over and roll it out on that side. Continue to slide and unstick with the pastry scraper until the dough is too thin and large to move without tearing it. At that point, continue rolling without the help of the pastry scraper until the dough is $1/8$ inch thick.

To transfer the dough into a pie pan, slide the pastry scraper underneath the sides of the dough, then firmly and swiftly lift it by one edge and fold the circle in half. Using the pastry scraper, fold the half in half so that the crust is in quarter-folds. Lift the folded dough into the plate (I use the pastry scraper for this too), placing the triangular point in the center of the plate. With your hands, firmly and swiftly unfold the dough so it drapes evenly over the plate, gently tucking it into the bottom. Top crusts are even easier to place—just follow these instructions to drape the dough over the filling.

On Edges

Trim edges 1 inch past the lip of the pie plate before folding them under. Failure to do so may result in par-baked, too-thick pie crust.

On Your Cold Hands

Cold hands, warm heart.

On Your Warm Hands

It's okay. As long as they aren't sweaty. If they are, use flour as a gymnast would use chalk.

On Torn, Smashed, Shattered, or Otherwise Messed-Up Crust

The oven will heal all.

A Recipe for Pie Crust

As taught to the author by a wise baker. Makes dough for one double crust pie.

2 $^1/_2$ cups of flour
1 tablespoon sugar
1 teaspoon salt
8 tablespoons lard
8 tablespoons butter
ice water

To learn how to make pie, observe pie makers and imitate the methods that seem most graceful, grace being the sort of efficiency that hides its usefulness with beauty. My mother's panicked flip of rolled-out dough into the plate, for example, I abandoned long ago, though I'll never relinquish the nostalgia of her conviction that when it came to pastry, anything could go wrong at any time. But I'm getting ahead of myself. Start with water.

It must be clean. It must be icy. Freeze about a cup and a half in a spouted liquid measure while you prepare the rest of the recipe.

When it comes to pie, our hands are our best tools. We are not woodworkers; we do not need hammers and saws. We are not accountants; math will tell us how many servings, not how to make or serve them. We are pianists. Cut your nails, and if you paint them, make sure the varnish doesn't flake off and disappear into your dough.

In a large metal bowl, mix flour, salt, and sugar. Cut tablespoon-sized chunks of butter and lard and drop them into the flour. Toss the fat with the flour to evenly distribute it.

Position your hands palms up, fingers loosely curled, the same way you relax your hand above your head while falling asleep. Scoop up flour and fat and rub it between your thumb and fingers, letting it fall back into the bowl after rubbing it. Do this, reaching into the bottom and around the sides to incorporate all flour into fat until the mixture is slightly yellow, slightly damp. The mixture should be chunky—mostly pea sized with some almonds and walnuts. The smaller bits should resemble coarse damp sand.

Get the water. Pour it in a steady thin stream around the bowl for about ten seconds. Toss to distribute the moisture. You'll probably need to pour more water and toss again. As the dough gets close to perfection, it will become a bit shaggy and slightly tacky to the touch. Press a small bit of the mixture together and toss it gently in the air. If it breaks apart, add more water, toss to distribute moisture, and test again. If the dough ball keeps its shape, it's done.

Gather the dough in two balls with firm, brief pressure. Quickly mold the dough into thick discs using your palms and thumbs. Wrap the dough in plastic. Refrigerate for an hour to three days before rolling.

Remember that patience requires virtue, but pie only requires patience.

A Master Recipe for Fruit Pie

Fruit pie filling has five essential ingredients: fruit, sugar, salt, spice, and thickener.

Fruit. Of all our materials, fruit is the most variable. Consider season, consider color, consider ripeness and scent. Consider sweetness, tartness, and texture. Consider pectin. Choose the best fruit. Always. Know how to tell a blue nub of paste from a blueberry, a ball of sand from an apple, a rock from a peach.

Sugar. Unless baking for children, go easy on the sugar. You'll figure out how much you need by pouring on a $1/2$ cup, tasting, pouring on another 1/4 cup, tasting, and so on. The sweeter the fruit, the less sugar you'll need. Try using brown and white sugar combinations, or honey, or maple syrup. Again, go by taste. The most sugar I ever use is 1 $1/4$ cup for rhubarb pie. The least is $1/2$ cup, for a maple blueberry pie. I use 3/4 cup for just about everything else.

Salt. Just a pinch. One for every pie.

Spice. Go easy on it. Many recipes call for a stiff dose of cinnamon and nutmeg, perhaps because they have assumed that you bought bad fruit. You did not. You bought good fruit. Don't over-spice it. A pinch of nutmeg is often all you need.

Many fillings benefit from the juice of half a lemon. Citrus clarifies sweet and prevents fruit from browning. This is true for stone fruits, berries, apples, and pears especially. Some fillings benefit from vanilla or almond extract. Try $^1/_2$ to 1 teaspoon to see how you like it.

After adding sugar, salt, and spice to your pie filling, taste it. Do you need more lemon? Do you need more salt? More sugar? More spice? Add at will, but slowly, tasting as you go. Once your filling tastes exactly as you like it, add thickener.

Thickener. Specifically flour, butter, and pectin. Pectin is a natural thickener that reduces the need for flour. When present, beware gummy pie. When absent, beware soupy pie. Compensate accordingly with 2-8 tablespoons of flour.

Quince, apples, and pears have a lot of natural pectin. Quince has the most; pears the least. Pies made with these fruits or a mixture of them need only 2-3 tablespoons of flour and 2 tablespoons of butter cut into small chunks and scattered on top of the filling before you put the top crust on. Grated apples can be used to firm up low-pectin fruits like berries. Sour cherries can have a lot of pectin too. They need about 5 tablespoons of flour.

Berries and stone fruit have very low pectin content. That's why berry and peach pies have a bad habit of turning into fruit soup. Thicken those fillings with 5-8 tablespoons of flour. If the fruit is fresh and not too juicy, I'll use 5 tablespoons. If it's very juicy, 6-8 tablespoons.

Wheat flour, tapioca flour, and cornstarch are all acceptable thickeners. My favorite is tapioca flour. It forms a thick but not jammy sauce that stays bright after cooking and is completely tasteless. Flour can sometimes lighten the sauce in strange ways, and sometimes you can taste it, but it is a dependable thickener. Cornstarch I can often taste, so I rarely use it.

Once you've added thickener, stir it gently into the fruit and mound the filling in a pie shell. If you're using wheat flour, dot the filling with 2-3 tablespoons' worth of butter chunks. If you're using tapioca flour or cornstarch, no extra butter is necessary.

Place the top crust over all, trim excess dough, crimp the edge, cut vents, and place the whole thing in the refrigerator or freezer to chill while your oven heats.

Start the pie at 425 degrees. Right before placing the pie in the oven, brush the top crust (but not the edge) with milk or an egg white wash and sprinkle sugar over all.

Bake on 425 for 10 to 15 minutes. When the crust is blond and blistered, turn the oven down to 375 degrees. Bake for another 40 to 50 minutes. Most pies need 55-60 minutes to bake fully, longer if you've used frozen fruit. You'll know the pie is done when the top crust is golden brown and the juices bubble slowly at the edge. The juices should look viscous—but just at the edge! If they do not look viscous or they're boiling briskly, or if both of these things are true, put the pie back in. Check on it in five minutes.

Cool the pie on a wire rack so air can circulate to the bottom crust.

Some people believe in hot pie. They don't care if the filling sets up, so they cut a piece right away. The rest of us wait for an hour or two—an ingenious way to force family time—before cutting the first slice.

Apple Pie

As American as what? In colonial times, apple pie was the harried housewife's peanut butter and jelly sandwich. Children and apples were plentiful; pastry is tastier than uninvented tupperware; and pie is still the only food that holds itself.

1 double crust pie dough recipe

5 Gravenstein apples (or 2 McIntosh and 3 Granny Smith)
1 almost-ripe Bartlett pear
3/4 cup mild honey (better quality is better)
juice of half a lemon (about one tablespoon)
1/2 teaspoon cinnamon
big pinch nutmeg
pinch salt
3 tablespoons flour
2 tablespoons chilled unsalted butter, cut into small pieces
1 egg white
1 teaspoon water
demerara sugar

Make the dough and refrigerate it for at least an hour, or overnight. Roll out the bottom crust and place it in a 9 or 10-inch pie plate. Tuck the crust into the plate and trim the edges, then refrigerate it while you prepare the rest of the pie. Preheat the oven to 425 degrees.

Heat the honey in a small saucepan on medium low heat until it flows freely. While the honey warms up, core and slice the apples and pears to $1/4$ inch thickness. Add the lemon juice and sprinkle the salt and spices over the fruit. Pour the honey over all and gently combine. Taste and adjust spice, sweet, and lemon as needed. Add the flour and stir again, then set filling aside.

Roll out the top crust. Pour the filling into your bottom crust. If there is too much liquid to fit in the pan with the apples, fill the pan not quite to the rim with juice and set the rest of it aside. Smooth the filling into a mound with your hands and dot it with small pieces of butter. Place the top crust on the pie. Crimp the crust into an upstanding ridge and make generous steam vents. In a small bowl, whisk together the egg white and teaspoon of water, then brush the crust with the egg white wash and sprinkle demerara sugar over everything.

Bake for 10 to 15 minutes until the crust is blond and blistered. Rotate the pie front to back and reduce the heat to 375 degrees. Bake until bubbling, 40 to 50 minutes.

Cool on a wire rack at least an hour before serving.

Mumbleberry Pie

The mumbleberry is an imaginary fruit used by bakers who can't remember what they've put in their berry pies. This version uses a grated top crust—an ideal option if you're using frozen dough, especially if you also can't remember how long ago you froze it.

1 double crust pie dough recipe

1 cup rhubarb sliced $1/2$ inch thick
1 cup blueberries
1 cup strawberries
1 cup sour cherries
1 cup blackberries (or some other mystery combo of 5 cups fresh or frozen fruit)
1 cup sugar
juice of half a lemon (about one tablespoon)
big pinch of nutmeg
pinch salt
$1/3$ cup tapioca flour
demerara sugar

Make the dough. Refrigerate one half and freeze the other for at least an hour, or overnight. Roll out the bottom crust and place it in a 9 or 10-inch pie plate. Tuck the crust into the plate, trim the edges, and fold them into an upstanding ridge. Refrigerate the crust while you prepare the rest of the pie. Preheat the oven to 400 degrees.

In a large bowl, combine the fruit, sugar, lemon juice, nutmeg, and salt. Toss gently to mix. Taste and adjust spice, sweet, and lemon as needed. Sift the tapioca flour over the mixture and toss gently to mix again. Turn the filling into the chilled bottom crust and smooth it with your fingers.

Using the largest holes of a box grater, grate the frozen top crust dough over the pie as if it were a block of cheese. Use a fork to move the crust gratings for even coverage and cooking. Sprinkle demerara sugar over the top crust. Bake the pie on the center oven rack for 10-15 minutes, or until the crust is blond and blistered. Then turn the oven down to 375 degrees. Turn the pie front-to-back so that it browns evenly and slip a rimmed baking sheet under it so juices don't make a mess of your oven. Bake until the top is golden brown and the juices bubble thickly, about 40 to 50 minutes--possibly longer if you used frozen fruit.

Cool on a wire rack at least an hour before serving.

Cherry Rhubarb Pie

You were expecting strawberry, right? Though the seasons of these two fruits are mismatched, (rhubarb in spring, cherries in summer) a forkful of this sweet-tart treat will surprise the jaded pie eater. As if there is such a thing.

1 double crust pie dough recipe

2 1/2 cups of rhubarb sliced 1/2 inch thick
2 1/2 cups fresh or frozen sour cherries
1 cup sugar
pinch nutmeg
pinch salt
1 teaspoon almond extract
1/3 cup flour
2 tablespoons unsalted butter, cut into small pieces
1 egg white
1 teaspoon water
demerara sugar

Make the dough and refrigerate it for at least an hour, or overnight. Roll out the bottom crust and place it in a 9 or 10-inch pie plate. Tuck the crust into the plate and trim the edges, then refrigerate it while you prepare the rest of the pie. Preheat the oven to 425 degrees.

In a large bowl, combine the fruit, sugar, nutmeg, salt, and almond extract. Toss gently to mix. Taste and adjust spice and sweet as needed. Sift the flour over the mixture and toss gently to mix again. Set aside while you roll out the top crust.

Turn the filling into the chilled bottom crust and smooth it with your fingers. Dot the top of the pie filling with butter. Drape the top crust over the filling. Crimp the crust into an upstanding ridge and make generous steam vents. In a small bowl, whisk together the egg white and teaspoon of water, then brush the crust with the egg white wash and sprinkle demerara sugar over everything.

Bake at 425 degrees for 10 to 15 minutes until the crust is blonde and blistered. Rotate the pie front to back and reduce the heat to 375 degrees. Bake until bubbling, about 40 to 50 minutes. Cool on a wire rack at least an hour before serving.

Maple Blueberry Pie

This pie is the last thing Violet Beauregarde tasted before Willie Wonka's experimental chewing gum turned her into a blueberry.

$^1/_2$ of a double crust pie dough recipe

For the crumble:
$^3/_4$ cup all-purpose flour
$^3/_4$ cup rolled oats (not quick-cooking)
$^1/_3$ cup brown sugar
$^1/_2$ teaspoon cinnamon
$^1/_4$ teaspoon salt
1 stick of cold unsalted butter, cut into $^1/_2$ inch chunks

For the filling:
4 cups blueberries (fresh or partially thawed)
$^1/_2$ cup high-quality maple syrup
juice of half a lemon (about one tablespoon)
$^1/_4$ teaspoon ground cinnamon
pinch salt
$^1/_3$ cup tapioca flour

Make the dough and refrigerate it for at least an hour, or overnight. Roll out the bottom crust and place it in a 9 or 10-inch pie plate. Tuck the crust into the plate, trim the edges, and fold them into an upstanding ridge. Refrigerate the crust while you prepare the rest of the pie. Preheat the oven to 400 degrees.

Measure the flour, oats, brown sugar, cinnamon, and salt into a food processor and pulse to combine. Add the chunked butter to the mixture. Combine with ten to fifteen one-second pulses until the mixture resembles coarse sand. Refrigerate while preparing the filling.

In a medium bowl, combine the blueberries, maple syrup, lemon juice, cinnamon, and salt. Taste and adjust spice, sweet, and lemon as needed, then add the tapioca flour and stir gently to combine. Turn the filling into the chilled pie shell, smoothing the fruit with a spoon. Bake in the center of the oven on 400 degrees for 25 minutes.

Remove the pie from the oven and spread the top with all of the oat crumble. It should cover the blueberries completely and be about 1/4 inch thick. Return the pie to the oven and bake on 350 degrees for 25 to 30 minutes until the crumble is toasted and brown and the blueberry juices bubble thickly at the edge—possibly longer if you used frozen fruit. Transfer the pie to a wire rack and let cool for at least an hour before serving.

Peach Ginger Pie

Once a woman entered a pie contest. It was her first. She was nervous. Absolutely sure she wouldn't win, was a fool for trying. She dropped off her pie at the event, ran home, and hid. A full day passed before she heard the news: her peach ginger pie had won Best in Show. I was a fool, *she thought.* Running is good exercise, but not when it's away from the thing you want.

1 double crust pie dough recipe

5 large, ripe peaches or 7 medium (or 5 to 6 cups of frozen sliced peaches)
3/4 cup clover honey
2 tablespoons peeled and finely chopped fresh ginger
juice of half a lemon (about one tablespoon)
big pinch of powdered ginger
pinch of nutmeg
pinch of cayenne pepper
pinch of salt
1/3 cup tapioca flour
1 egg white
1 teaspoon water
demerara sugar

Make pie dough and refrigerate for at least an hour. Preheat the oven to 425 degrees. Roll out the bottom crust and place it in a 9 to 10-inch pie plate. Tuck the dough into the plate, trim the edges, and refrigerate while preparing the filling and top crust.

Combine honey and fresh chopped ginger in a small saucepan and heat on low for 20 minutes. While the honey is warming up, pit, peel, and slice the peaches so they're about $1/4$ inch thick. Put the slices in a large bowl and squeeze the lemon over them. Add the powdered ginger, nutmeg, cayenne pepper, and salt. Pour the heated honey and fresh ginger over all. Mix gently until the honey and spices are evenly distributed, then taste and adjust sweet, spice, and lemon as needed. Sprinkle tapioca flour over the peaches and mix gently again.

Roll out the top crust. Retrieve the bottom crust from the refrigerator. Pour the filling into your bottom crust. If there is too much liquid to fit in the pan with the peaches, fill the pan not quite to the rim with juice and set the rest of it aside. Smooth the filling into a mound with your hands. Place the top crust over the filling. Trim off any excess dough and fold an upstanding ridge. Cut large steam vents. In a small bowl, whisk together the egg white and teaspoon of water, then brush the crust with the egg white wash and sprinkle the demerara sugar over everything.

Bake on 425 degrees for 10 to 15 minutes until the crust is blistered and blond. Rotate the pie 180 degrees to assure even baking, then lower the temperature to 375 degrees and bake for another 50 to 60 minutes until the crust is golden and the juices start to bubble slowly at the edge—possibly longer if you've used frozen fruit.

Cool on a wire rack for at least an hour before serving.

How to Eat Pie

1. With a fork and plate.

   Preferred by polite company and mothers speaking to children.

2. With your hands.

   Preferred by breakfasting couples, hurried working girls, and barbecue attendees.

3. With your face.

   Preferred by the fat kid, the skinny kid, the kid with sinus problems from winning pie eating contests, performance artists, and ambushed politicians.

4. With a spoon.

   Preferred by people who do not do their dishes often and consequently are out of forks.

5. With someone else's hands.

   Preferred by children, lovers, and invalids.

What phrase best describes your thoughts on pie?

a) "Don't go into Mr. McGregor's garden: your father had an accident there; he was put into a pie."
> — Beatrix Potter

b) "A triangle of pie is the best way ever discovered to round out a square meal."
> — The Farm Journal's Complete Pie Cookbook

c) "Promises and pie crust are made to be broken."
> — Jonathan Swift

d) "A boy doesn't have to go to war to be a hero; he can say he doesn't like pie when he sees there isn't enough to go around."
> — Edgar Watson Howe

e) "When someone asks if you'd like cake or pie, why not say you want cake and pie?"
> — Lisa Loeb

Thank you

To my mother, for teaching me how to bake.
To my father, for teaching me how to work.
To both of them, for teaching me how to love.

This book began as part of a collaborative sculpture project with Brian Schoneman in the winter of 2010. It grew under the editorial care of Jennifer Borges Foster, became a letterpressed zine thanks to Rosanna Kvernmo, and matured into a book with the encouragement and advice of Heather McHugh, David Shields, Richard Kenney, Kristen Millares Young, Elissa Ball, Kary Wayson, Katherine Eulensen, Elizabeth Colen, Piper Daniels, Heather Malcolm, Jessica Lynn Bonin, Brian McGuigan, Jory Mickelson, Becca Yenser, Sam Ligon, Alice Acheson, my cohort at the University of Washington, and my recipe testers, especially Josie Friedman. The wise baker is Kate McDermott.

To all of you, to Bruce Rutledge and Chin Music Press, to Chelsey Slattum and Natalie Shields, to Nick Lebo and Gail Orcutt and Lisa Walz, to Richard Hugo House, Centrum, Artist Trust, and 4Culture, and to everyone who bought the zine and believed in this manuscript long before it had a perfect spine:

Thank you.

Kate Lebo makes poems and pies in Seattle, Washington. Her writing has appeared in *Best New Poets, Gastronomica,* and *Poetry Northwest* among other journals, and she's currently at work on a pie cookbook for Sasquatch Books, forthcoming in 2014. She teaches creative writing at Richard Hugo House and pie making at Pie School, her cliche-busting pastry academy. For poems, pies, and other tasty treats, visit katelebo.com.

Jessica Lynn Bonin works in a multitude of mediums. A painter and illustrator by trade, she lives in a bend in the road called Edison, Washington, where she runs a shop called the Lucky Dumpster. Past clients include DASH Design (NYC), the World Bank, and National Parks. She is a member of PUNCH Gallery in Seattle, Washington. See more of her work at jessicalynnbonin.com.

Notes

Notes

Notes

Notes